MIGHTY MACHINES

AIRCRAFT CARRIERS

BY RYAN NAGELHOUT

 Gareth Stevens
PUBLISHING

HOT TOPICS

Please visit our website, www.garethstevens.com. For a free color catalog of all our high-quality books, call toll free 1-800-542-2595 or fax 1-877-542-2596.

Nagelhout, Ryan.
 Aircraft carriers / Ryan Nagelhout.
     pages cm. — (Mighty military machines)
 Includes index.
 ISBN 978-1-4824-2106-4 (pbk.)
 ISBN 978-1-4824-2105-7 (6 pack)
 ISBN 978-1-4824-2107-1 (library binding)
 1. Aircraft carriers—United States—Juvenile literature. I. Title.
 V874.3.N34 2015
 623.825'50973—dc23

                              2014024264

First Edition

Published in 2015 by
Gareth Stevens Publishing
111 East 14th Street, Suite 349
New York, NY 10003

Copyright © 2015 Gareth Stevens Publishing

Designer: Nicholas Domiano
Editor: Ryan Nagelhout

Photo credits: Cover background Ensuper/Shutterstock.com; series logo Makhnach_S/ Shutterstock.com; cover, pp. 1, 5, 8, 19, 23, 25 Stocktrek/Stocktrek Images/Getty Images; p. 6 Ramon Espelt Photography/Shutterstock.com; p. 7 Marty Lederhandler/APphotos.com; p. 9 Universal History Archive/Universal Images Group/Getty Images; pp. 10, 22 Joe Raedle/ Getty Images News/Getty Images; p. 11 Thoms J. Abercrombie/National Geographic/Getty Images; p. 12 Keystone-France/Gamma-Keystone/Getty Images; p. 13 Planet News Archive/ SSPL/Getty Images; p. 14 Topical Press Agency/Hulton Archive/Getty Images; p. 15 U.S. Navy/APphotos.com; p. 16 Hulton Archive/Getty Images; p. 17 Popperfoto/Getty Images; p. 20 Dorling Kindersley/Getty Images; p. 21 Pool/Getty Images News/Getty Images; p. 24 Giovanni Colla/Stocktrek Images/Getty Images; p. 27 Mass Communication Specialist Second Class Aidan P. Campbell/Navy.mil; p. 29 Jose Gil/Shutterstock.com; p. 30 aurin/ Shutterstock.com.

Printed in the United States of America

CPSIA compliance information: Batch # **CW15GS**: For further information contact Gareth Stevens, New York, New York at 1-800-542-2595.

CONTENTS

MIGHTY CARRIERS

The **military** uses many different kinds of ships. These boats and subs travel all over the world doing different jobs. The biggest of these mighty machines are called aircraft carriers.

Older ships are decommissioned when a navy is no longer using them.

Aircraft carriers are boats used in a navy, or the part of a military that works at sea. Many countries have at least one aircraft carrier in their navy. The United States Navy has the most by far.

An aircraft carrier is like a floating airport! Airplanes, jets, and helicopters take off and land on the **flight deck**. Lots of different people and machines work together on an aircraft carrier. Carriers have many levels and millions of parts.

US aircraft carriers are so big they're considered US territory when in international waters.

HOME AT SEA

An aircraft carrier does more than take care of airplanes. It's home to thousands of sailors. It can stay at sea for months and months. An aircraft carrier has its own hospital, barbershop, and post office!

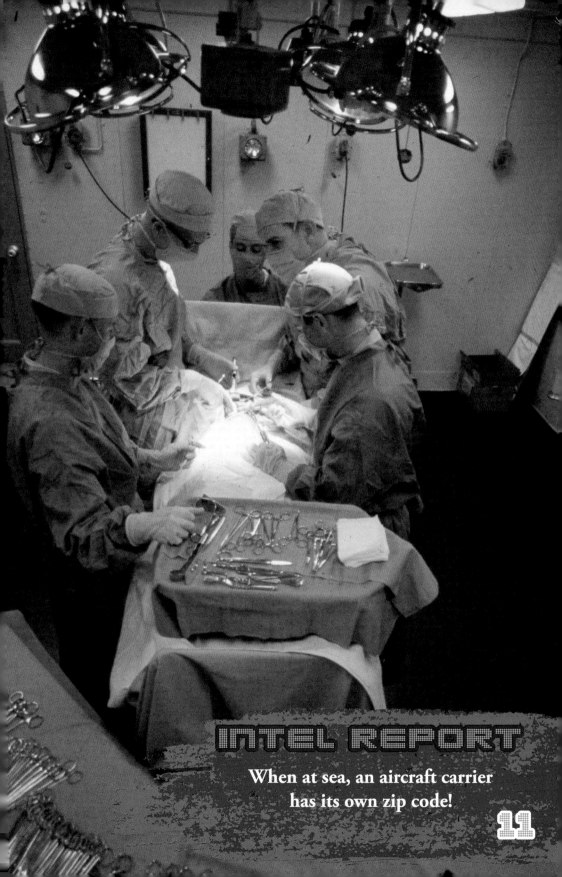

11

The first aircraft carriers were just regular ships. In 1910, a **civilian** pilot named Eugene Ely took off from a wooden deck on the USS *Birmingham*. The next year, Ely landed on a deck atop the USS *Pennsylvania*.

INTEL REPORT

Ely's plane flew 2.5 miles (4 km) to shore, but not before skipping on the water and damaging its propeller.

13

THE LANGLEY

In 1922, the USS *Jupiter* was made into the first aircraft carrier. Renamed the USS *Langley*, it first had planes take off and land on it while in Virginia. The *Langley* was officially made active in 1924.

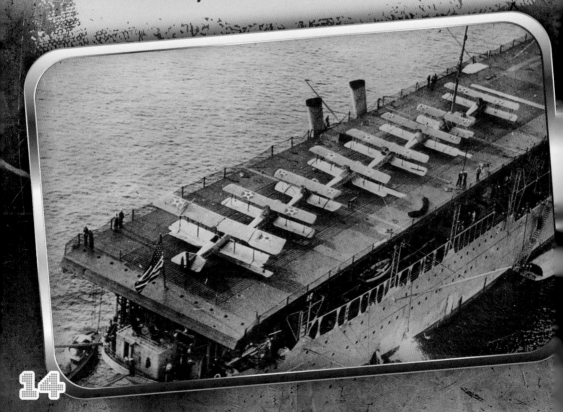

The USS *Langley* sank in 1942 when it was attacked by Japan during World War II.

15

Aircraft carriers have changed in many ways. **Fleet** carriers used in World War II led war efforts in the Pacific and the Atlantic Oceans. They acted as bases of operation and helped countries carry out attacks far from land.

INTEL REPORT

The United States added more than 20 aircraft carriers to its navy during World War II.

Modern aircraft carriers are gigantic ships with lots of different moving parts. The US Navy has two different classes of aircraft carrier, the Nimitz class and the Enterprise class. The *Enterprise* first set sail in 1961. The Nimitz class was introduced in 1975.

INTEL REPORT

Because of their gigantic size, aircraft carriers can only travel about 35 miles (56 km) per hour.

LOTS OF LEVELS

Both Enterprise and Nimitz class carriers have many levels. The flight deck is where planes take off and land. The island towers over the flight deck. It's where people control the ship and help planes take off and land.

Many levels on an aircraft carrier, including the engine room, are well below the water level.

MOVING PLANES

Planes and helicopters are stored in the huge hangar below the flight deck. Sailors bring planes to the flight deck using big elevators. Many people work on the flight deck to move planes around.

INTEL REPORT

Enterprise and Nimitz carriers can
hold about 60 planes in their hangar.

There isn't much room to take off or land on a carrier. Some planes use a **catapult** to help them take off. Others need help landing. Some planes use a **tailhook** to catch on to strong wires that help the plane stop.

THE TAILHOOK

INTEL REPORT

The flight deck only has about 500 feet (152 m) of space to land a plane on.

THE FORD CLASS

The newest aircraft carriers are part of the Ford class. These ships each have 25 decks and cost $12 billion. The first Ford class carrier is called the *Gerald R. Ford* CVN 78.

INTEL REPORT

The Ford class will replace the Enterprise and Nimitz class aircraft carriers.

THE FUTURE

Ford carriers are made to help planes take off much faster. They'll also help the navy save money. Aircraft carriers are sure to be part of the military for years to come!

THE FLIGHT DECK

ISLAND

ELEVATORS

CATAPULTS

JET BLAST
DEFLECTORS

FOR MORE INFORMATION

Books

Bodden, Valerie. *Aircraft Carriers*. Mankato, MN: Creative Education, 2012.

Hamilton, John. *Aircraft Carriers*. Minneapolis, MN: ABDO Publishing, 2012.

Tagliaferro, Linda. *Who Lands Planes on a Ship? Working on an Aircraft Carrier*. Chicago, IL: Raintree, 2011.

Websites

The Aircraft Carrier
navy.mil/navydata/ships/carriers/carriers.asp
This official US Navy site contains a complete history of its aircraft carriers.

Aircraft Carrier Strength
globalfirepower.com/navy-aircraft-carriers.asp
This website lists which nations have aircraft carriers in their navy.

The Ford Class
thefordclass.com/design.html
Learn more about the future of aircraft carriers in the US Navy.

GLOSSARY

catapult: a machine for getting an airplane into the air at flying speed very quickly

civilian: a person not on active duty in the military

decommission: to take a ship out of service

fleet: a group of warships

flight deck: the top deck of an aircraft carrier where planes take off and land

international waters: ocean territory not controlled by any one country

military: relating to the armed services

tailhook: a hook on a plane used to catch wires to help it land on an aircraft carrier

World War II: a war fought from 1939 to 1945 that involved countries around the world

INDEX